EASY LITTLE PEPPERS

Elissa Milne

This book is dedicated to my first piano teacher, Mavis Francis, who encouraged my earliest experimentings.

© 2004 by Faber Music Ltd
First published in 2004 by Faber Music Ltd
Bloomsbury House 74–77 Great Russell Street London WC1B 3DA
Music processed by MusicSet 2000
Cover illustration by Dave Wood
Printed in England by Caligraving Ltd

ISBN10: 0-571-52313-7
EAN13: 978-0-571-52313-9

To buy Faber Music publications or to find out about the full range of titles available
please contact your local music retailer or Faber Music sales enquiries:

Faber Music Limited, Burnt Mill, Elizabeth Way, Harlow, CM20 2HX England
Tel: +44 (0)1279 82 89 82   Fax: +44 (0)1279 82 89 83
sales@fabermusic.com   fabermusicstore.com

FABER *ff* MUSIC

CONTENTS

TO THE TEACHER

Elissa Milne's *Little Peppers* series is a graded sequence of exciting performance pieces designed to introduce beginner pianists to essential technical skills. For more details and a CD of complete performances, see the *Guided tour of the Little Peppers*: ISBN 0-571-52332-3.

NOTE ON PLAYING *PEAS IN A POD*

Peas in a pod has been composed in eight equal parts so you can enjoy arranging the music yourself. You can play these parts in any order, miss out a part or play each more than once – though bear in mind that parts I and IV are not ideal to finish with. This means that your version of *Peas in a pod* might be much shorter than in this book, or even much longer!

What's more, because all the parts work well with each other, you can play this piece as a duet (two players on one piano), a duo (two players on two pianos), or even with three or four people playing simultaneously! Each player should start on a different part; experiment until you find your favourite combination. Alternatively, you may want to try playing the piece straight through as written; in which case, it will work simultaneously with the *Peas in a pod* from any of the other *Little Peppers* books! Whatever you decide, have fun with creating your own *Peas in a pod*.

SUNSHOWER

Elissa Milne

GROOVY MOVIE

HOCUS POCUS

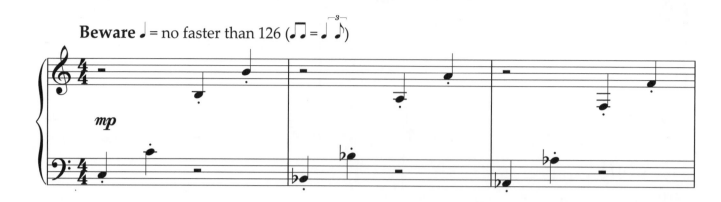

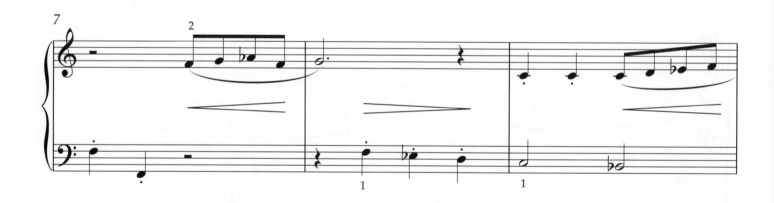

WAKE UP

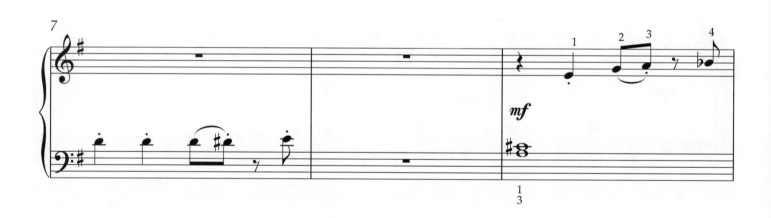

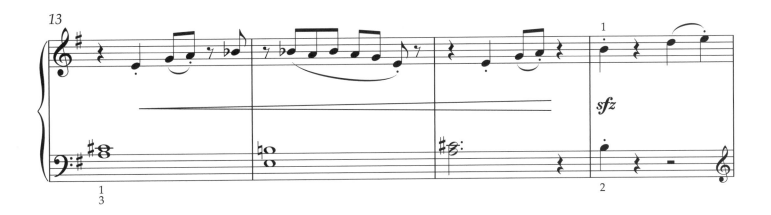

CAT AND MOUSE

Ready to pounce and nervous! ♩ = 168-184

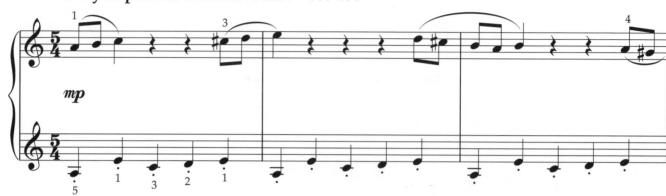

MOZZIE

Persistently ♩ = 138

WHO'S BEEN BOUNCING ON MY BED?

THE LONE ECHIDNA

An echidna is an Australian animal with spikes, somewhat like a hedgehog.

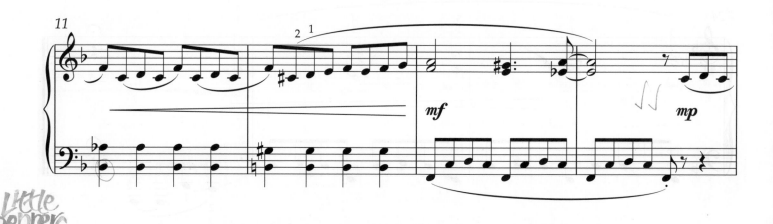

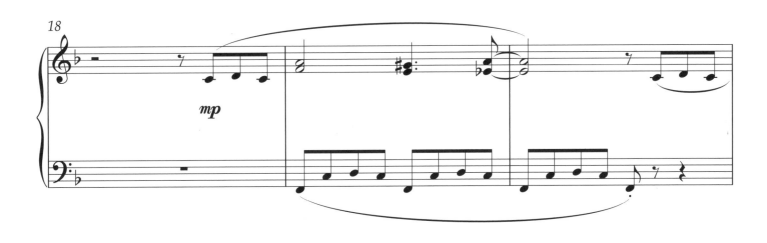

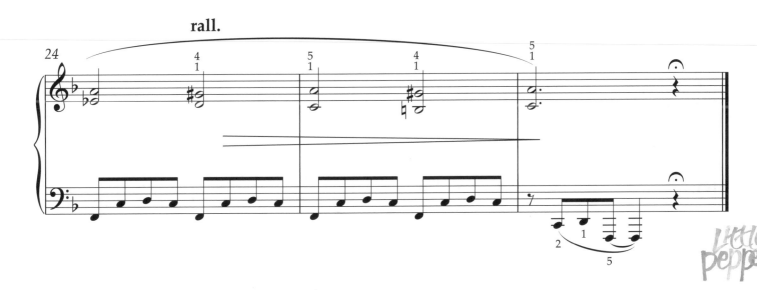

STARLIGHT

Wishful ♩ = 80

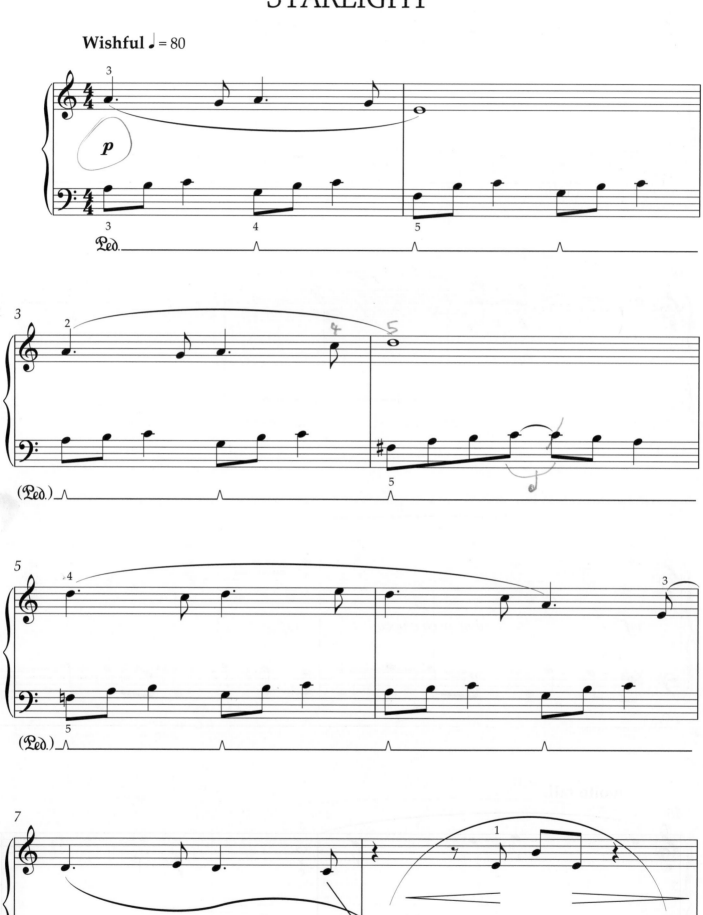

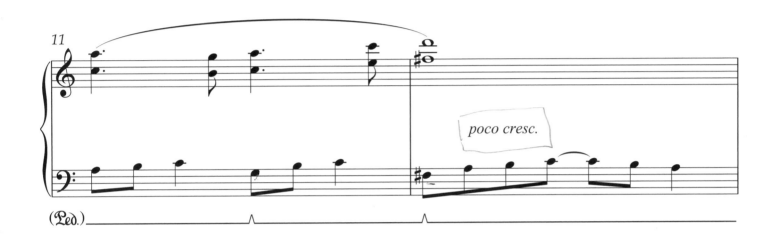

poco cresc.

molto rall.

CAT'S WHISKERS

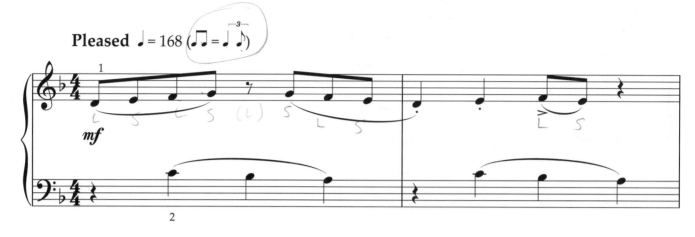

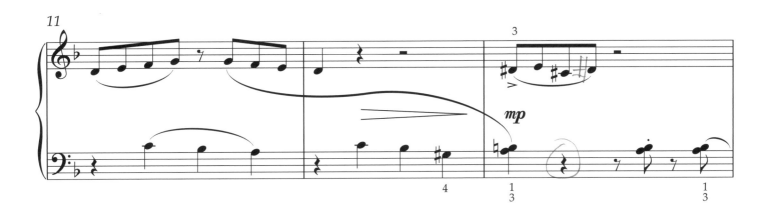

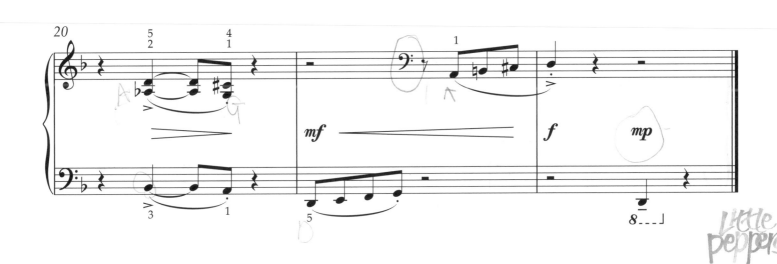

BANDICOOT BALLET

A bandicoot is a rabbit-like animal with a long tail and a pouch in which to keep its babies.

Scampering ♩ = 100-120

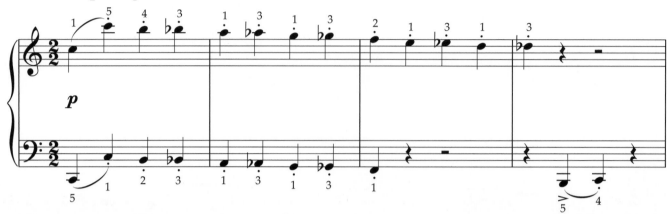

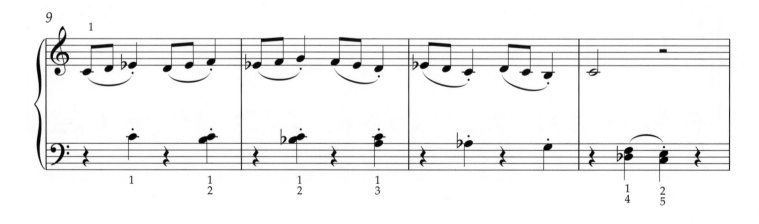

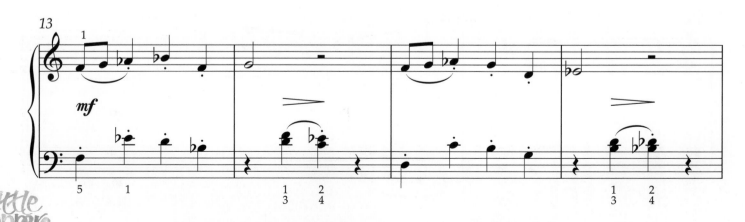

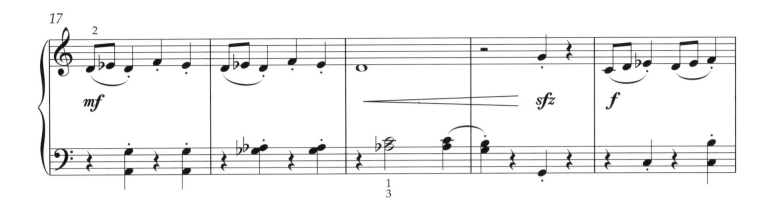

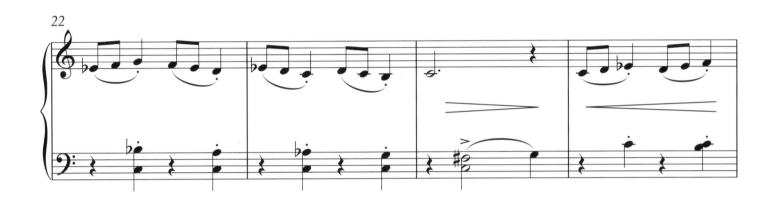

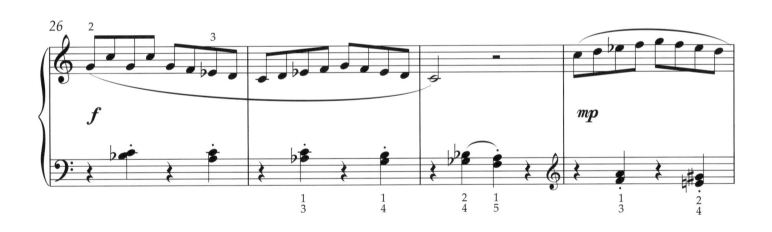

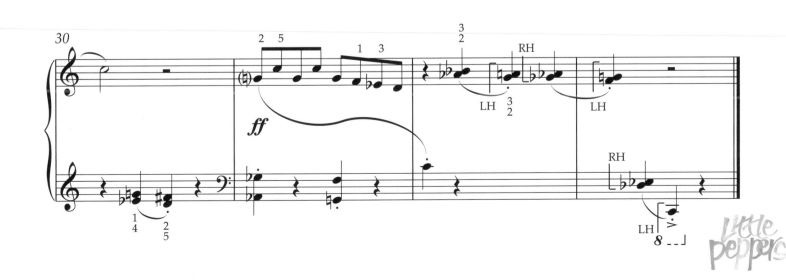

PEAS IN A POD *

* See page 2 for a note on how to play this piece. Page 24 may be photocopied to avoid page turns.
† Play only when continuing to Section II, VI or VII.